牛油果
滑稽动作

MANDARIN

MARCY SCHAAF

AVOCADO
ANTICS
MARCY SCHAAF

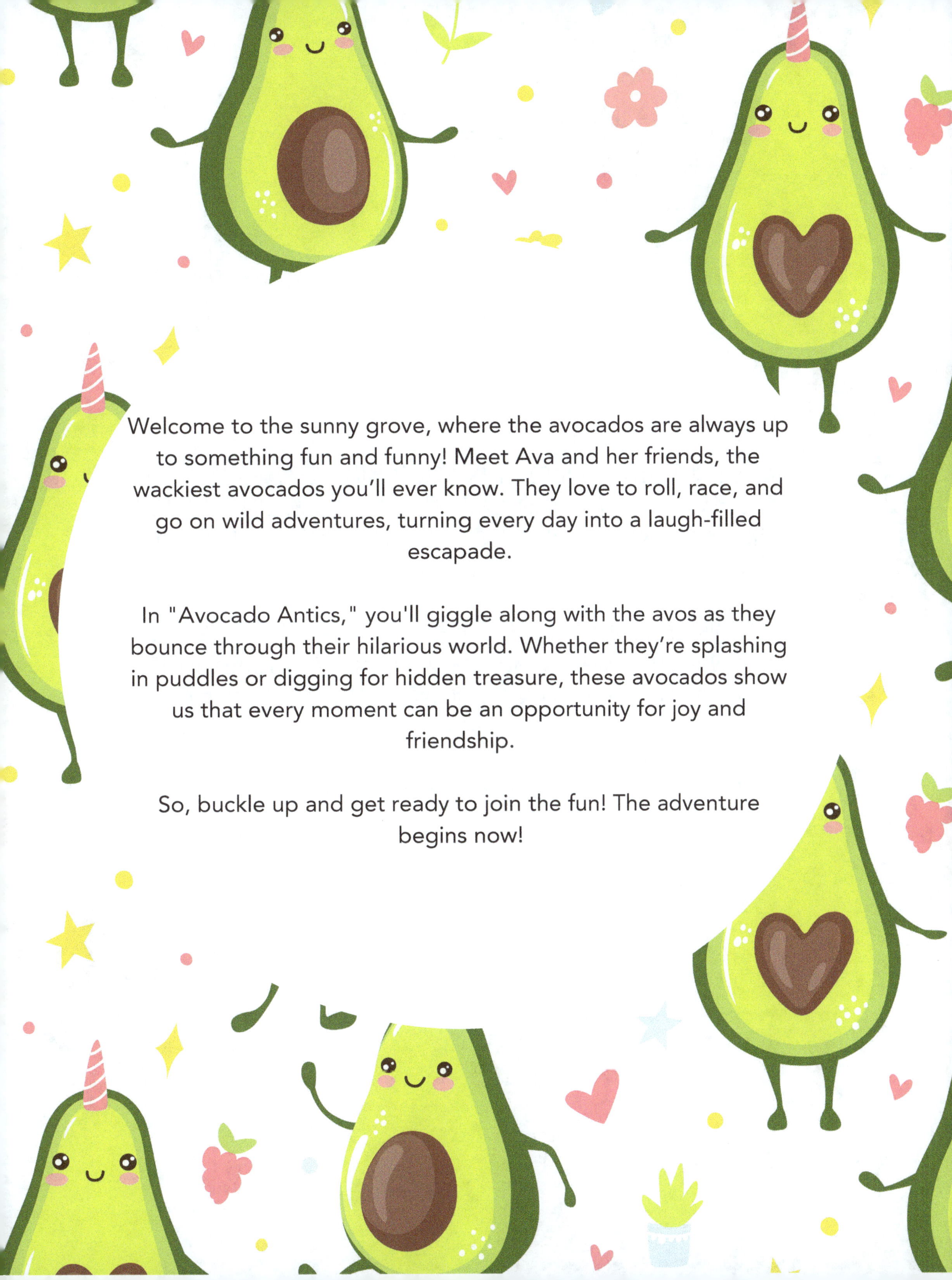

Welcome to the sunny grove, where the avocados are always up to something fun and funny! Meet Ava and her friends, the wackiest avocados you'll ever know. They love to roll, race, and go on wild adventures, turning every day into a laugh-filled escapade.

In "Avocado Antics," you'll giggle along with the avos as they bounce through their hilarious world. Whether they're splashing in puddles or digging for hidden treasure, these avocados show us that every moment can be an opportunity for joy and friendship.

So, buckle up and get ready to join the fun! The adventure begins now!

欢迎来到阳光林，这里的牛油果总是会做出一些有趣又好玩的事情！来认识一下艾娃和她的朋友们吧，她们是你见过的最古怪的牛油果。她们喜欢滚动、赛跑和进行野外探险，把每一天都变成充满欢笑的冒险。

在"牛油果滑稽动作"中，您会和牛油果一起咯咯笑，因为它们在搞笑的世界中蹦蹦跳跳。无论是在水坑里嬉戏还是挖掘隐藏的宝藏，这些牛油果都向我们展示了每一刻都可以成为欢乐和友谊的机会。

所以，系好安全带，准备加入这场乐趣吧！冒险现在就开始！

Copy Write @ Marcy Schaaf 2024
Avocado Antics

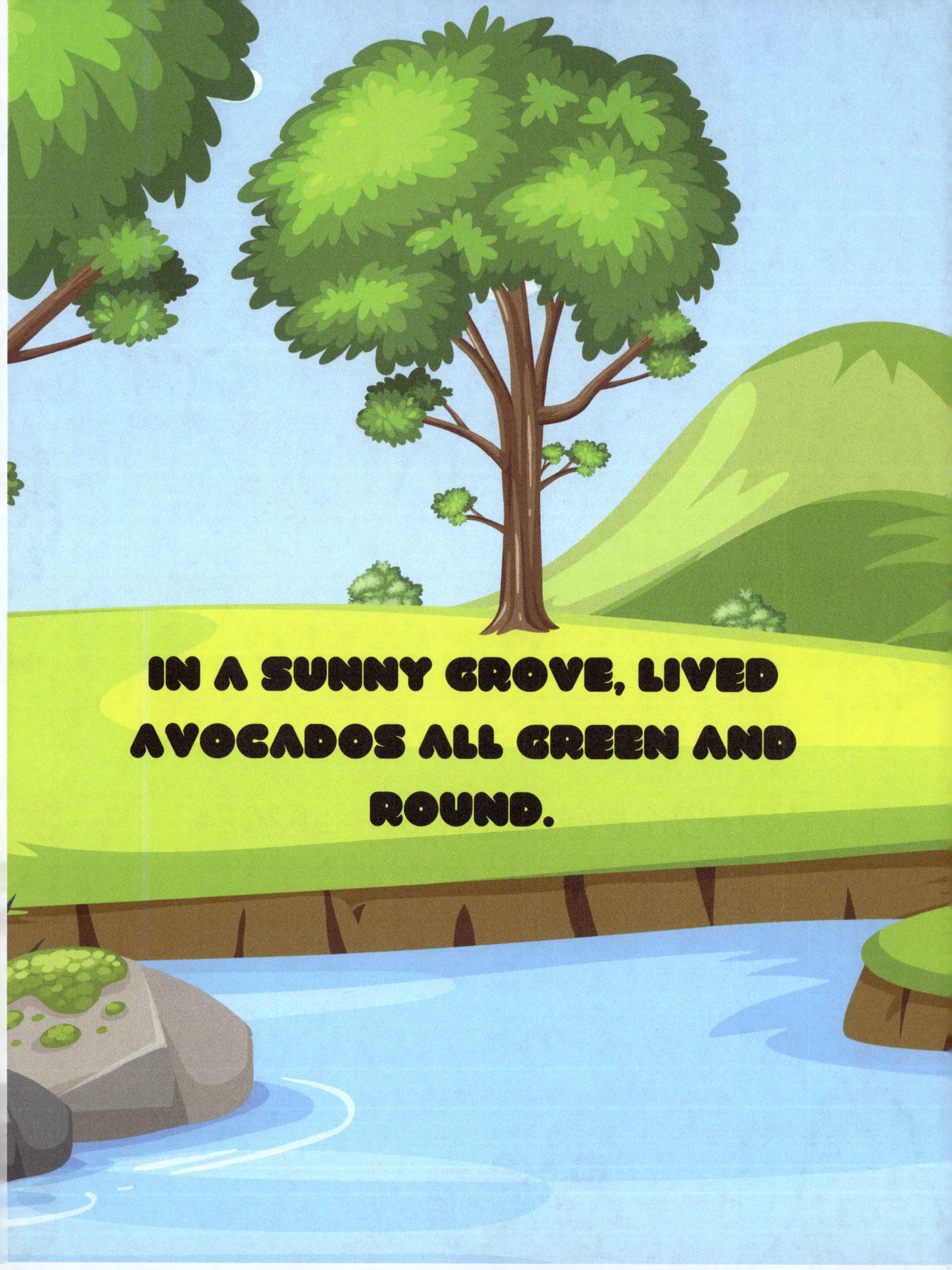
IN A SUNNY GROVE, LIVED
AVOCADOS ALL GREEN AND
ROUND.

阳光明媚的树林里，长着又绿又圆的鳄梨。

THEY LOVED TO PLAY AND
LAUGH, MAKING SILLY SOUNDS.

他们喜欢玩耍、大笑，发出傻傻的声音。

ONE DAY, AVA, THE SMALLEST AVOCADO, HAD A GREAT IDEA.

有一天，最小的鳄梨艾娃有了一个好主意。

"LET'S HAVE A RACE" SHE SAID, WITH A SMILE EAR TO EAR.

"我们来比赛一下
吧。"她笑容满面地说
道。

GIGGLES AND CHEERS FILLED THE AIR, A JOYOUS SOUND.

笑声和欢呼声响彻云霄，充满欢乐
的声音。

AVOS LINED UP, READY TO ROLL,
BOUNCING ON THE GROUND.

Avos 排好队，准备滚动，在地上弹
跳。

AVA SHOUTED, "GO!" AND OFF THEY WENT, ROLLING FAST.
GO

艾娃喊道：“走！”他们就出发了，
飞快地滚动着。
去

BUT THEN THEY HIT A BUMP,
FLYING HIGH, WHAT A BLAST!

但后来它们撞上了一个凸起，飞得很高，真是爆炸啊！

THEY LANDED IN A PUDDLE, SPLASHING EVERYWHERE.

它们掉进了水坑，水花四溅。

COVERED IN MUD, THEY
LAUGHED WITHOUT A CARE.

他们满身泥巴，却无忧无虑地大笑。

THEY CLEANED UP IN THE SUN
NO TIME TO SPARE.

他们赶紧在阳光下进行清理工作。

AVA SAID, "THAT WAS THE BEST DAY EVER!"

艾娃说："那是我一生中最美好的一天！"

THE AVOS AGREED, "WE WILL FORGET IT NEVER!"

牛油果爱好者们表示同意，“我们永远不会忘记它！”

PLAYING GAMES AND SINGING SONGS, HAVING FUN.

玩游戏、唱歌，玩得很开心。

THE FUNNY AVOCADOS, ALWAYS
FOUND A WAY.

有趣的鳄梨，总能找到办法。

TO TURN EVERY MOMENT, INTO
A PERFECT DAY.

把每一刻都变成完美的一天。

ONE MORNING, THEY FOUND A MYSTERIOUS BOX.

一天早上，他们发现
了一个神秘的盒子。

INSIDE WERE COSTUMES, SHOES,
AND COLORFUL SOCKS.

里面有服装、鞋子和五颜六色的袜
子。

THEY DRESSED UP AS PIRATES,
WITH HATS AND A PATCH.

他们打扮成海盗，戴
着帽子和补丁。

PRETENDING TO FIND TREASURE, THEY STARTED TO HATCH.

它们假装找到宝藏，开始孵化。

THEY DUG IN THE DIRT, WITH
SHOVELS AND GLEE.

他们兴高采烈地用铲子挖着泥土。

FINDING A HIDDEN CHEST
BENEATH A BIG TREE.

在一棵大树下找到一个隐藏的箱子。

INSIDE WERE JEWELS, SHINY
AND BRIGHT.

里面全是珠宝，闪闪发光。

THEY DANCED AND TWIRLED, IN THE MOONLIGHT.

他们在月光下跳舞、旋转。

SO WHENEVER YOU FEEL, A
LITTLE BIT BLUE.

所以无论何时，你都会感到有点忧郁。

REMEMBER THE AVOCADOS, AND THEIR LAUGHTER TOO.

还记得鳄梨，还有它们的笑声。

AS THE STARS TWINKLED, THEY WHISPERED GOODNIGHT.

星星闪烁，低声说着晚安。

DREAMING OF NEW
ADVENTURES, UNTIL MORNING
LIGHT.

梦想着新的冒险，直到晨曦来临。

Books By Schaaf

www.BookBySchaaf.com

Find us at: